YAHWEH, A GOD OF VIOLENCE?
Understanding Justice, Retribution and the Character of God in the Old Testament

YAHWEH, A GOD OF VIOLENCE?

Understanding Justice, Retribution and the Character of God in the Old Testament

Harold Palmer

LOGOS LIGHT

YAHWEH, A GOD OF VIOLENCE?
Understanding Justice, Retribution and the Character of God in
the Old Testament

ISBN (13) (Paperback): 978-1-68109-028-3
ISBN (10) (Paperback): 1-68109-028-7
ISBN (13) (Kindle): 978-1-68109-029-0
ISBN (10) (Kindle): 1-68109-029-5
ISBN (13) (ePub): 978-1-68109-030-6
ISBN (10) (ePub): 1-68109-030-9

LOGOS LIGHT

LogosLight™
an imprint of TellerBooks™
TellerBooks.com/LogosLight

t TellerBooks

www.TellerBooks.com

Manufactured in the U.S.A.

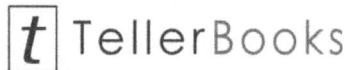

NOTE: Unless otherwise stated herein, all biblical Scriptures quoted herein are taken from the New King James Version or American Standard Version translations.

DISCLAIMER: The opinions, views, positions and conclusions expressed in this volume reflect those of the individual author and not necessarily those of the publisher or any of its imprints, editors or employees.

ABOUT THE IMPRINT

The LogosLight™ imprint first started with the collection The Church Fathers Speak, a compilation of the voices of the early Church fathers and their teachings on sanctity and Christ-like living. This ancient wisdom guides the reader on the path to cultivating holiness that yields self-dominion, patience, and virtue.

LogosLight has since grown to encompass Christian poetry and inspirational books, translations of the Bible and Hebrew Scriptures, and various Christian records and Liturgies.

LogosLight books also examine the role of Judeo-Christian thought on the formation of Western civic institutions, the moral foundations of just societies, and the role of faith in civil governance.

LOGOS LIGHT

CONTENTS

ABBREVIATIONS

English Translations of the Bible:

ASV................American Standard Version
BBE................Bible in Basic English
Darby.............Darby Bible
ESV ....English Standard Version
ISV ....International Standard Version
KJV ....King James Version
MKJV............Modern King James Version
NIV ....New International Version
NKJV ....New King James Version
RSV...............Revised Standard Version

Books of the Bible:

1Ch.................1 Chronicles
1Co.................1 Corinthians
1Jn.................1 John
1Ki.................1 Kings
1Pe.................1 Peter
1Sa.................1 Samuel
1Th.................1 Thessalonians
1Ti.................1 Timothy
2Ch.................2 Chronicles
2Co.................2 Corinthians
2Jn.................2 John
2Ki.................2 Kings
2Pe.................2 Peter
2Sa.................2 Samuel
2Th.................2 Thessalonians
2Ti.................2 Timothy
3Jo.................3 John
Acts ....Book of Acts
Amos.............Book of Amos
Col.................Colossians

Dan.................Daniel
Deu.................Deuteronomy
Ecc.................Ecclesiastes
Eph.................Ephesians
Est ....Esther
Exo ....Exodus
Eze.................Ezekiel
Ezr.................Book of Ezra
Gal.................Galatians
Gen.................Genesis
Hab.................Habakkuk
Hag.................Haggai
Heb.................Hebrews
Hos ....Hosea
Isa.................Isaiah
Jas.................James
Jer.................Jeremiah
Job.................Book of Job
Joel ....Book of Joel
John.................Gospel of John
Jon.................Jonah
Jos ....Joshua
Jude ....Book of Jude
Jdg.................Judges
Lam ....Lamentations
Lev ....Leviticus
Luke ....Gospel of Luke
Mal ....Malachi
Mark.................Gospel of Mark
Mat ....Gospel of Matthew
Mic ....Micah
Nah.................Nahum
Neh.................Nehemiah
Num.................Numbers
Oba.................Obadiah
Phm ....Philemon
Php ....Philippians
Pro ....Proverbs

Psa...................Psalms
Rev ....Revelation
Rom................Romans
Ruth................Book of Ruth
Son ....Song of Solomon
Tit....................Titus
Zec..................Zechariah
Zep ....Zephaniah

CHAPTER 1. INTRODUCTION

Genocide, infanticide, the destruction of entire peoples—these are among the acts of violence commanded or condoned by Yahweh, the God of the Old Testament. Examples abound throughout the Pentateuch and beyond of violence perpetrated by the Israelites at the beckoning of God. Entire cities and peoples, including Sodom, Gomorrah, Jericho, Amalek and Midian, are destroyed directly or indirectly by God. The Israelites are commanded to "kill both man and woman, infant and nursing child, ox and sheep, camel and donkey'" (1Sa 15:1-3). God instructs the Israelites to "conquer and utterly destroy [and] show no mercy to" seven nations (Deu 7:1-2) and to "put to death everyone in the cities, men, women, and dependents" and leave no survivor in Heshbon (Deu 2:31-34).

Can we conclude from these examples that Yahweh is a brutal god of war and violence? Is Yahweh's character incompatible with that of Jesus, who in the Sermon on the Mount teaches His disciples to "not resist an evil person," "turn the other cheek," "love your enemy" and "pray for those who persecute you" (Mat 5:38-44)?

Some commentators have concluded from the Old Testament's war accounts that Yahweh is a petty god with an insatiable blood thirst. In this study, Harold Palmer rejects and refutes these conclusions by approaching the question from a completely fresh angle. He sees the destruction of entire peoples not as a reflection of God's character, but as a reflection of *man's* character. Cities and peoples are destroyed as a natural consequence of their sins, with those having put their faith in Yahweh, such as Rahab, spared from the fate that befalls their community.

The starting point for this study is thus that man was created by God for a purpose and to abide by a moral code. When that code is broken, man, having rebelled against and fallen short of God's perfect moral law, is separated from God. The consequence of this separation is death, and its antidote is the gift of grace, perfected by Christ on the cross.

CHAPTER 2. UNDERSTANDING YAHWEH THROUGH THE LENS OF SCRIPTURE

A. "THE WAGES OF SIN IS DEATH"

One can only understand the Christian Scriptures through the guidance of the Holy Spirit. Without this guidance, one will see only a dreadful, destructive God. For example, without a Scriptural perspective on sin, salvation, and God's mercy, one will read the many plagues that God struck on the Egyptians, as well as the killing of Egyptian babies as recorded in the book of Exodus,[1] as evidence of a violent, cruel God. However, when one approaches the Scriptures with the understanding that there is "not a righteous man on earth who does what is right and never sins"[2] and that "the wages of sin is death,"[3] one can only conclude that all are under the curse of sin and deserve death for their sins. Within this context, God's destruction of entire peoples, including small children, in the Old Testament, is simply the meting out of His justice. In contrast, the great works he commits for the salvation of Israel are demonstrations of his bountiless love and mercy.

---

[1] Exodus 12:29-30.
[2] Ecc 7:20.
[3] Rom 6:23.

B. IS IT FAIR THAT A WHOLE PEOPLE SHOULD BE DESTROYED FOR THE SINS OF SOME? THE META-NARRATIVE

Throughout the OT, we read about the Israelites' destruction of entire peoples, generally as punishment to these people for idolatry, attacking the Israelites, or impeding the Israelites from the promised land. Many of those who are destroyed are often women and children, including infants and nursing children (see, *e.g.*, 1Sa 15:3). Obviously, not all of those who were killed were responsible for the sins being punished. For example, a nursing child cannot be guilty of the idolatry of his fathers, as such a child is not yet even at the age of conscience. Is it fair that all of these people, including the innocent, be punished for the sins of some?

The only way around this conundrum is as follows: mankind is doomed by sin to death. The only escape from death is through faith in God. Faith is salvific.

Out the sea of man's sin, rebellion, and faithlessness, there arose Abraham, a man of faith. We read of Abraham's faith in obeying when "he called to go out to the place which he would receive as an inheritance,"[4] of his dwelling in the "land of promise" by faith,[5] and of his obedience in offering up Isaac, his "only begotten son," by faith.[6]

The Israelites' blessings came as a result of Abraham's faith. All of the other peoples, including the children, were condemned to death because they did not have faith in the one true God because they were not in Abraham's covenant.

---

[4] Heb 11:8.
[5] Heb 11:9.
[6] Heb 11:17.

CHAPTER 3. GOD'S DESTRUCTION OF PEOPLES IS NOT GENOCIDE BECAUSE IT IS NOT BASED ON ETHNICITY

God destroys indiscriminately of race or ethnicity; his destruction is based on sin alone.

A. GOD PUNISHES EVEN HIS OWN PEOPLE

1. Plague as Punishment for Worshipping the Gods of the Midianites (Num 25)

While in Acacia Grove, the Israelites "began to commit harlotry with the women of Moab" and bow down to their gods (Num 25:1-2), thus arousing the Lord's anger (Num 25:3). The Lord commended Moses to hang the offenders (Num 25:4). Numbers 25 describes a plague of Israel that was only stopped after Phinehas thrust his javelin through an Israeli and a Midianite woman who he presented to his brethren (Num 25:6-8). The focus of God was not on Israeli versus non-Israeli, but rather with those flirting with foreign gods and idolatry.

2. The Israeli Men of War (Jos 5)

To demonstrate that God's destruction is not based on race, Joshua narrates that He destroyed Israel's own "men of war" because of their sinfulness (Jos 5:6):

> For the children of Israel walked forty years in the wilderness, till all the people who were men of war, who came out of Egypt, were consumed, because they did not obey the voice of the LORD—to whom the LORD swore that He would not show them the land which the LORD had sworn to their fathers that He would give us.

This is not, however, to deny God's own favor of the Jewish nation. However, it must be conceded that the Israelites, like the Gentiles, are under God's judgment.

3. Punishment of Jerusalem for the Evils of Jehoiakim and Jehoiachin (2Ch 36)

Second Chronicles reports another instance of the Lord's anger against Jerusalem. When Jehoiakim was made king over Judah and Jerusalem, "he did evil in the sight of the LORD his God" (2Ch 36:5) and he committed "abominations" (2Ch 36:8). His son Jehoiachin then reigned in his place and "did evil in the sight of the LORD" (2Ch 36:9). Jehoiakim's brother Zedekiah then reigned over Judah and Jerusalem and "did evil in the sight of the LORD his God, and did not humble himself before Jeremiah the prophet, who spoke from the mouth of the LORD" (2Ch 36:12). "Moreover all the leaders of the priests and the people transgressed more and more … and defiled the house of the LORD which He had consecrated in Jerusalem" (2Ch 36:14). Although the Lord sent warnings to His people (2Ch 36:15), they "mocked the messengers of God, despised His words, and scoffed at His prophets" (2Ch 36:16). The Lord was thus stirred to anger and "He brought against them the king of the Chaldeans, who killed their young men with the sword in the house of their sanctuary, and had no compassion on young man or virgin, on the aged or the weak; He gave them all into his hand" (2Ch 36:17).

4. The Punishments of Jerusalem (Eze 9)

Just as not all in Jericho were destroyed, but rather, the harlot Rahab was spared for having protected the spies, so too were the righteous of the Israelites spared when God ordered the punishment of Jerusalem for its "abominations" and for "fill[ing] the land with violence" and "provok[ing God] to anger" (Eze 8:17). God commands that "those who have charge over the city draw near, each with a deadly weapon in his hand" (Eze 9:1), and that one of them "Go through … Jerusalem, and put a mark on the foreheads of the men who sigh and cry over all the abominations that are done within it" (Eze 9:4) and that the others "Go after him … and kill" (Eze 9:5), utterly slaying "old and young men, maidens and little children and women; but do not come near anyone on whom is the mark" (Eze 9:6).

This thus shows that God is violent not only with the non-Israelites, but with the Israelites as well. It is important to note that God puts to death not only the little children of the pagans, but the little children of the Israelites as well (Eze 9:6).

B. A WOMAN OF FAITH IN JERICHO AND HER FAMILY ARE SPARED: THE STORY OF RAHAB (JOS 2, 6)

1. Biblical Account of the Destruction of Jericho and Salvation of Rahab (Jos 2, 6)

a. Rahab and the Two Israeli Spies (Jos 2)

Joshua sent out two men to spy Jericho. They went, and came to the house of a prostitute named Rahab, where they lodged (Jos 2:1). The King of Jericho was told that men came from Israel to spy the land (Jos 2:2). So the King sent to Rahab and ordered her to bring out the men who came to her (Jos 2:3). Rahab hid the two men on the roof with stalks of flax (Jos 2:4, 6) and said that the

men had already left (Jos 2:5). Then the men pursued them and the
gate was shut behind them (Jos 2:7). Rahab went up to the men on
the roof (Jos 2:8) and said to them,

> I know that the Lord has given you the land and that all the
> inhabitants of the land are terrified of you (Jos 2:9), for we have
> heard how the Red Sea was dried when you came out of Egypt
> and how you destroyed the two kings of the Amorites on the
> other side of the Jordan (Jos 2:10); your God is the God in
> heaven above and on earth below (Jos 2:11). Since I have shown
> you kindness, I beg you that you show kindness to my father's
> house (Jos 2:12) and spare my father, mother, brothers, sisters
> and all that they have and deliver us from death (Jos 2:13).

The men obliged her request if none of her household speak of
what they were doing (Jos 2:14). Then she let them down by a rope
through the window from the city wall (Jos 2:15). They told her
that their oath would only be valid if she brought her family into
her home and bound a line of scarlet cord in the window through
which she let them down (Jos 2:18) and if she did not speak of
their plans to anyone (Jos 2:20).

The two men returned to Joshua and told him what had
happened (Jos 2:23).

b. Destruction of Jericho; Salvation of Rahab and Her Household
    (Jos 6)

Jericho was all shut up because the Israelites let no one go out
or come in (Jos 6:1). The Lord said to Joshua, I have given into
your hands Jericho with its king and soldiers (Jos 6:2). Let your
soldiers make a circle round the town, going around it once for six
days (Jos 6:3). Have seven priests go before the ark with seven
trumpets in their hands. On the seventh day, you are to go around
the town seven times, the priests blowing their trumpets (Jos 6:4).
At the sound of a long note on the trumpets, let the people give a

loud cry; and the wall of the town will come down and all the people are to go straight forward (Jos 6:5).

Then Joshua instructed the priests to up the ark of the covenant and for seven priests to take seven trumpets in their hands (Jos 6:6). The seven priests with their trumpets went forward before the Lord, blowing on their trumpets and the ark of the covenant went after them (Jos 6:8).

Joshua had the ark go all around the town and back to the tents the first six days (Jos 6:11-14). At dawn on the seventh day, they went around the town (Jos 6:15) and on the seventh time, at the sound of the priests' horns, Joshua said, Give a loud cry (Jos 6:16); the city and all who are in it are doomed for destruction; only Rahab the harlot and her household shall live (Jos 6:17).

So the people gave a loud cry and the trumpets were sounded and the wall came down flat, so that the people went up into the town, every man going straight before him, and they took the town (Jos 6:20). They destroyed every living thing in it: men and women, young and old, ox and sheep and donkeys (Jos 6:21).

The two spies went in and brought out Rahab and her household and left them outside the camp of Israel (Jos 6:23) and burned the city with fire (Jos 6:24). Joshua spared Rahab and her household, who dwells in Israel to this day (Jos 6:25).

2. Analysis

Although Rahab was a part of the people of Jericho, she was not destroyed with them because of her faith in the God of Israel. Believing the God of the spies to be the "God in heaven above and on earth beneath" (Jos 2:11), Rahab hid the spies from the king's men and saved them. As a result of her kindness (Jos 2:12), the men promise, "Our lives for yours, if none of you tell this business of ours. And it shall be, when the LORD has given us the land, that we will deal kindly and truly with you" (Jos 2:14). Joshua later said to the people, "Now the city shall be doomed by the LORD to destruction, it and all who are in it. Only Rahab the harlot shall live, she and all who are with her in the house, because she hid the messengers that we sent" (Jos 6:17). After the blowing of the trumpets and the shout of the people, Jericho's city wall fell (Jos 6:20) and the Israelites "utterly destroyed all that was in the city" (Jos 6:21), save Rahab and her family (Jos 6:22-23).

However, it is important to note here that it was not God who commanded the sparing of the harlot Rahab, but rather, the spies who promised it and Joshua who respected their word. Nonetheless, as God is sovereign, one can draw from the destruction of Jericho and salvation of Rahab that even a Canaanite harlot, who but for her faith that the God of the Israelites was the true God, was unrighteous, can be saved from destruction through faith.

CHAPTER 4. GOD'S DESTRUCTION OF PEOPLES AIMED AT PUNISHING SIN

A. SODOM AND GOMORRAH DESTROYED FOR THEIR SIN; TEN RIGHTEOUS PEOPLE WOULD HAVE SPARED SODOM (GEN 18-19)

1. Biblical Account

a. Abraham's Plea with God not to Destroy Sodom (Gen 18)

Because the outcry against Sodom and Gomorrah was great, and because their sin was very grave, God went down to see whether their acts were as bad as the outcry that rose against them (Gen 18:20-21). Abraham then pled with God not to destroy Sodom, saying, Would You also destroy the righteous with the wicked? Suppose there were fifty righteous in the city; would You not spare the city? (Gen 18:23). God said that he would spare all of Sodom if he found within the city fifty righteous people (Gen 18:26), forty five (Gen 18:28), forty (Gen 18:29), thirty (Gen 18:30), twenty (Gen 18:31), or ten (Gen 18:32).

b. Two Angels Visit Lot and Warn Him to Flee the City; the Men of Sodom Wish to Lay with the Angels (Gen 19)

While Lot was sitting in the gate of Sodom, he saw two angels come and bowed himself with his face to the ground (Gen 19:1) (these were angels that God sent to destroy the city). They were going to spend the night in the open square, but Lot insisted that they spend the night at his home. They agreed (Gen 19:2-3).

That night, old and young men of Sodom came to Lot's home (Gen 19:4), asking Lot to bring out the angels so they could know them carnally (Gen 19:5). Lot refused and instead offered them his daughters (Gen 19:7-8). The men sought to break down the door (Gen 19:9), but the angels struck them with blindness (Gen 19:11).

The angels warned Lot to flee the city (Gen 19:12), as God sent them to destroy it (Gen 19:13). Lot warned his sons in law, but they did not believe him (Gen 19:14). In the morning, the angels urged him to flee and took him, his wife and his two daughters by the hands to set them outside of the city (Gen 19:15-16). Then one of them told them to flee and not look back (Gen 19:17).

c. Lot Flees to Zoar; Sodom and Gomorrah Destroyed; Lot's Wife Becomes a Pillar of Salt (Gen 19)

The angels permitted Lot to flee to a nearby city which was called Zoar (Gen 19:19-22). God sent fire and brimstone from heaven (Gen 19:24) and destroyed Sodom and Gomorrah and all of their inhabitants (Gen 19:24-25). While Lot's wife fled with them, she looked back and became a pillar of salt (Gen 19:26).

2. Analysis

We thus learn the following lessons from the Genesis account of Sodom and Gomorrah:

-   The cities were destroyed because their sin was very grave (Gen 18:20). Several books of the Bible give an account of the nature of the sins of Sodom: Jeremiah, highlighting the sins of Jerusalem (adultery, lies, strengthening the hands of evildoers, non-repentance), compares the city to Sodom and Gomorrah (Jer 23:14); Ezekiel writes, "this was the iniquity of your sister Sodom: She and her daughter had pride, fullness of food, and abundance of idleness; neither did she strengthen the hand of the poor and needy" (Eze 16:49). The Genesis account gives a clear illustration of the sins of Sodom: The men of Sodom came to Lot's home (Gen 19:4), asking Lot to bring out the angels that Lot had welcomed into his home so they could know them carnally (Gen 19:5). When Lot refused, they yelled, "stand back!" and nearly broke down his door (Gen 19:9). So strong was their desire to violate Lot's home and have homosexual relations with the angels that even Lot's offering them his daughters (Gen 19:7-8) did not placate them.

- The fact that God utterly destroyed Sodom and Gomorrah illustrates the extent of sin within the cities. Abraham rightly commented that it would be far from God, the "Judge of all the earth," to "slay the righteous with the wicked, so that the righteous should be as the wicked" (Gen 18:25). And as Abraham pled with God to not destroy Sodom, God said that he would spare the entire city if He found within the city fifty righteous people (Gen 18:26), forty five (Gen 18:28), forty (Gen 18:29), thirty (Gen 18:30), twenty (Gen 18:31) or even ten (Gen 18:32). The subsequent destruction of Sodom (Gen 19:24-25) indicates that not even ten righteous people could be found there.

- After Abraham pled with God, the angels that he invited to stay with him warned him to flee the city (Gen 19:12), as God sent them to destroy it (Gen 19:13). The fact that they gave him warning could be interpreted to mean that Lot, and perhaps also his wife and daughters who fled with him (Gen 19:15-16) were the only righteous in the entire city, and God did not intend to destroy the righteous with the unrighteous. Even Lot's sons-in-law did not believe him when he warned them (Gen 19:14), and they perished with the rest.

B. DESTRUCTION AS PUNISHMENT FOR BLOCKING THE PEOPLE OF GOD FROM REALIZING GOD'S WILL: HESHBON (DEU 2)

The Israelites "put to death everyone in the cities, men, women, and dependents" and "left no survivor" (Deu 2:31-34). This was a punishment to the people of Heshbon because their king Sihon would not let the Israelites pass through to inherit their land: "Sihon king of Heshbon would not let us pass through, for the Lord your God hardened his spirit and made his heart obstinate, that *He might deliver him into your hand, as it is this day*" (Deu 2:30).

C. DESTRUCTION AS PUNISHMENT FOR ATTACKING THE ISRAELITES

1. Bashan (Deu 3)

God's destruction of Bashan was as punishment for Bashan's attacking of the people of Israel (Deu 3:1-2). "So the LORD our God also delivered into our hands Og king of Bashan, with all his people, and we attacked him until he had no survivors remaining … utterly destroying the men, women, and children of every city" (Deu 3:3-6).

2. Amalek (1Sa 15)

The prophet Samuel gave Saul these instructions from the Lord: "The LORD sent me to anoint you king over His people, over Israel. Now therefore, heed the voice of the words of the LORD. Thus says the LORD of hosts: 'I will punish Amalek for what he did to Israel, how he ambushed him on the way when he came up from Egypt. Now go and attack Amalek, and utterly destroy all that they have, and do not spare them. But kill both man and woman, infant and nursing child, ox and sheep, camel and donkey'" (1Sa 15:1-3). This was as a punishment to Amalek for having assisted Eglon king of Moab against Israel (Jdg 3:12-13).

D. COMMANDING THE ISRAELITES TO ATTACK, HARASS, AND ULTIMATELY DESTROY AS A PUNISHMENT FOR HARASSING AND SEDUCING THE ISRAELITES: THE MIDIANITES (NUM 25)

After the Midianite women seduced the Israeli men at Peor, God commanded Moses to "Harass the Midianites, and attack them; for they harassed you with their schemes by which they seduced you in the matter of Peor and in the matter of Cozbi, the daughter of a leader of Midian, their sister, who was killed in the day of the plague because of Peor" (Num 25:17-18). The seduction of the Israelis led to a plague, and God sought to end the plague.

It is also important to note that Numbers 22:4-8 describes the complicity and co-conspiracy of the Midianites in joining the elders of Moab in trying to engage the services of the sorcerer Balaam in obtaining a curse against the Israelites. Though the Bible does not say so directly, the punishment levied against the Midianites in Num 25:17-18 may have also been due to these acts, which God ultimately thwarted by instead using Balaam to bless Israel.

God later commands Moses to "Take vengeance on the Midianites for the children of Israel. Afterward you shall be gathered to your people" (Num 31:2). Moses spoke to the people, telling them to "go against the Midianites to take vengeance for the LORD on Midian" (Num 31:3). The Israelites "killed the kings of Midian with the rest of those who were killed ... Balaam the son of Beor they also killed with the sword" (Num 31:8).

The Bible is not clear what this vengeance was for, but it is presumably the same that led God to command Moses to "Harass the Midianites, and attack them" in Numbers 25: the Midianites' seduction of the Israeli men. Moses tells the officers of the army: "Look, these women caused the children of Israel, through the counsel of Balaam, to trespass against the LORD in the incident of Peor, and there was a plague among the congregation of the LORD" (Num 31:16).

E. DESTRUCTION OF THE SEVEN NATIONS TO PREVENT THE ISRAELITES FROM ENGAGING IN THE IDOLATRY OF THEIR FOES (DEU 7)

In Deuteronomy 7, God instructs the Israelites to "conquer and utterly destroy [and] show no mercy to" (Deu 7:2) seven nations "greater and mightier than" Israel: "the Hittites and the Girgashites and the Amorites and the Canaanites and the Perizzites and the Hivites and the Jebusites" (Deu 7:1). This harsh treatment is commanded to the Israelites in order to prevent them from breaking the very first and most important commandment of God: "You shall have no other gods before Me" (Exo 20:3). For this reason, God later commands the Israelites to "destroy their altars, and break down their sacred pillars, and cut down their wooden images, and burn their carved images with fire" (Deu 7:5). Deuteronomy later makes clear why God instructed the Israelites to destroy these nations: to prevent the nations from teaching the Israelites "to do according to all their abominations which they have done for their gods, and you sin against the Lord your God" (Deu 20:18).

F. DESTRUCTION BECAUSE OF SINFUL ABOMINATIONS: THE CANAANITES OF JERICHO (JOS 6)

1. Scriptural Account

Jericho was all shut up because the Israelites let no one go out or come in (Jos 6:1). The Lord said to Joshua, I have given into your hands Jericho with its king and soldiers (Jos 6:2). Let your soldiers make a circle round the town, going around it once for six days (Jos 6:3). Have seven priests go before the ark with seven trumpets in their hands. On the seventh day, you are to go around the town seven times, the priests blowing their trumpets (Jos 6:4). At the sound of a long note on the trumpets, let the people give a loud cry; and the wall of the town will come down and all the people are to go straight forward (Jos 6:5).

Then Joshua instructed the priests to up the ark of the covenant and for seven priests to take seven trumpets in their hands (Jos 6:6). The seven priests with their trumpets went forward before the Lord, blowing on their trumpets and the ark of the covenant went after them (Jos 6:8).

Joshua had the ark go all around the town and back to the tents the first six days (Jos 6:11-14). At dawn on the seventh day, they went around the town (Jos 6:15) and on the seventh time, at the sound of the priests' horns, Joshua said, Give a loud cry (Jos 6:16). So the people gave a loud cry and the trumpets were sounded and the wall came down flat, so that the people went up into the town, every man going straight before him, and they took the town (Jos 6:20). They destroyed every living thing in it: men and women, young and old, ox and sheep and donkeys (Jos 6:21).

2. Reason for the Destruction of Jericho: The Canaanites' sin (Lev 18, 20; Deu 18)

a. Overview

Unlike the destruction of Heshbon, Bashan, Sodom, and many other nations, the reason for the destruction of the Canaanites in Jericho is not given in the Joshua 6 destruction text. On the basis of Joshua 6 on its own, it would seem that the only fault of the Canaanites is their very existence on land that God has promised to Israel. However, by reverting back to the Mosaic law given in the Pentateuch (*e.g.*, "according to the doings of the land of Canaan, where I am bringing you, you shall not do; nor shall you walk in their ordinances" (Lev 18:3)), one finds the reason for the destruction of Jericho: the sins of the Canaanites.

b. Leviticus 18

God warns the Israelites that if they commit any of the sins of those who were in the land before them—lying carnally with your neighbor's wife (Lev 18:20); letting your descendants pass through the fire to Molech (a god worshiped by the Canaanites and Phoenicians); profaning the name of your God (Lev 18:21); lying with a male as with a woman (Lev 18:22); mating with any animal (Lev 18:23); etc., the land would vomit them out. God thus warns the Israelites:

> "Do not defile yourselves with any of these things; for by all these the nations are defiled, which I am casting out before you. For the land is defiled; therefore I visit the punishment of its iniquity upon it, and the land vomits out its inhabitants" (Lev 18:24-25).
> "[F]or all these abominations the men of the land have done, who were before you, and thus the land is defiled, lest the land vomit you out also when you defile it, as it vomited out the nations that were before you" (Lev 18:27).

c. Leviticus 20

Leviticus 20 repeats the warning to the Israelites not to transgress God's law or engage in the abominations of the nation (the Canaanites of Jericho) that God would cast out before them:

> "You shall not walk in the statutes of the nation which I am casting out before you; for they commit all these things, and therefore I abhor them" (Lev 20:23).

d. Deuteronomy 12

Moses repeats the warning to the generation about to cross Jordan River and enter the promised land, warning them that He punishes nations for the evil that they do:

> "Take heed to yourself that you are not ensnared to follow them, after they are destroyed from before you, and that you do not inquire after their gods, saying, 'How did these nations serve their gods? I also will do likewise.' You shall not worship the Lord your God in that way; for every abomination to the Lord which He hates they have done to their gods; for they burn even their sons and daughters in the fire to their gods" (Deu 12:30-31).

Because Israel did not obey God but turned to idolatry and did the same abominations in the sight of God as the Canaanites, the nation was dispersed from the land. This is described in Psalm 106.

e. Deuteronomy 18

Deuteronomy 18 repeats the reason for the destruction of Jericho given in Leviticus 20: The sins of the Canaanites led to their destruction:

> Deu 18:9 "When you come into the land which the Lord your God is giving you, you shall not learn to follow the abominations of those nations.
> Deu 18:10 There shall not be found among you anyone who makes his son or his daughter pass through the fire, or one who

practices witchcraft, or a soothsayer, or one who interprets
omens, or a sorcerer,
Deu 18:11   or one who conjures spells, or a medium, or a
spiritist, or one who calls up the dead.
Deu 18:12 *For all who do these things are an abomination to
the Lord, and because of these abominations the Lord your God
drives them out from before you.*

3.   Faith in the God of the Israelites a Source of Salvation: The Story of Rahab (Jos 2, 6)

Furthermore, when viewed from the perspective of the biblical
metanarrative, one may say that Jericho deserved the destruction
that all sinners deserved. However, out of the sea of unbelief of
Jericho, one woman stood out as having faith in the God of Israeli:
Rahab, and through her faith, she and her family were saved. For
further discussion, *see* "A Woman of Faith in Jericho and Her
Family Are Spared: The Story of Rahab (Jos 2, 6)," *supra.*

4.   The Israelites Were Also Driven from the Land for their Sin

While the Israelites did not face the same wholesale destruction
that overcame the Canaanites, they were ultimately conquered and
driven from the land for their sin. After the Northern Kingdom
(Samaria) instituted idolatrous worship, it was conquered by the
Assyrians. After the Southern Kingdom (Judah) fell into sin, it was
overtaken by Babylon and the Jews were sent into exile. Jeremiah
repeatedly warned the Israelites that this fate would overcome
them; he prophesied the Babylonian captivity with these words of
God: "And you, even yourself, Shall let go of your heritage which
I gave you; And I will cause you to serve your enemies In the land
which you do not know; For you have kindled a fire in My anger
which shall burn forever" (Jer 17:4). He correctly prophesied that
the desolation of Jerusalem and servitude to the king of Babylon

would last seventy years (Jer 25:11), which came to pass from 586 to 516 BC.

The exile of Judah as a consequence of sin is further described in Psalm 106:

> Psa 106:34 They did not destroy the peoples, Concerning whom the Lord had commanded them,
>
> Psa 106:35 But they mingled with the Gentiles and learned their works;
>
> Psa 106:36 They served their idols, which became a snare to them.
>
> Psa 106:37 They even sacrificed their sons and their daughters to demons,
>
> Psa 106:38 And shed innocent blood, the blood of their sons and daughters, whom they sacrificed to the idols of Canaan; and the land was polluted with blood.
>
> Psa 106:39 Thus they were defiled by their own works, and played the harlot by their own deeds.
>
> Psa 106:40 Therefore the wrath of the Lord was kindled against His people, so that He abhorred His own inheritance.
>
> Psa 106:41 And He gave them into the hand of the Gentiles, and those who hated them ruled over them.
>
> Psa 106:42 Their enemies also oppressed them, and they were brought into subjection under their hand.
>
> Psa 106:43 Many times He delivered them; But they rebelled in their counsel, And were brought low for their iniquity.

CHAPTER 5. OTHER AFFLICTIONS AIMED AT PUNISHING SIN

A. PLAGUE IN ISRAEL AS A RESULT OF KING DAVID'S CENSUS (1CH 21)

Besides destroying entire peoples, God ordains other punishments as a result of sin. For example, in 1 Chronicles 21 we read of God's punishment of Israel because of David's sin in numbering (taking a census of) Israel. While the Scriptures are not particularly clear as to why this constituted a sin in God's eyes, it is clear that numbering Israel was not of God's will, since "Satan stood up against Israel, and moved David to number Israel" (1Ch 21:1). It is presumable that David numbered Israel out of lack of faith, and his belief that he could conquer Israel's enemies not by the power of God and trust in Him, but rather by Israel's numbers.

We read that "God was displeased with this thing" (1Ch 21:7) and He gave David a choice between three punishments: "either three years of famine, or three months to be defeated by your foes with the sword of your enemies overtaking you, or else for three days the sword of the LORD—the plague in the land, with the angel of the LORD destroying throughout all the territory of Israel" (1Ch 21:12). David chose the plague (1Ch 21:13).

B. KING UZZIAH'S LEPROSY AS A RESULT OF HIS BURNING INCENSE (2CH 26)

God blessed King Uzziah when he sought the Lord and did His will (2Ch 26). However, when Uzziah transgressed the Lord by burning incense in the temple (2Ch 26:16), an act that was reserved for the priests (sons of Aaron) (2Ch 26:18), leprosy broke out on his forehead (2Ch 26:19) and Uzziah was a leper until the day of his death (2Ch 26:21).

CHAPTER 6. VIOLENCE TO ENABLE THE ISRAELITES TO POSSESS THE PROMISED LAND AND PUT OFF THE PEOPLES TEMPTING THEM INTO IDOLATRY: THE PHILISTINES

The Philistines are the objects of God's wrath, punishment, and destruction throughout the Old Testament. Their plight as the arch-enemies of the Israelites in many ways parallels the plight of the modern-day Palestinians as the rivals of modern-day Israelis. We find many instances in which God commands the Israelites to drive the Philistines out of "Philistia" (Exo 23:31), destines the land of the Philistines to be possessed by the Israelites (Jos 13:1-2) and sends His Spirit upon Samson to bring death and destruction against the Philistines (Jdg 14:19; Jdg 15:15; Jdg 16:30).

Why were the Philistines the objects of this great wrath? They were sinners who not only engaged in idolatry, but also were a snare unto the Israelites and tempted them into their same sins. The Philistines are among the foreign peoples that tempt the Israelites into idolatry. We read: "Then the children of Israel again did evil in the sight of the LORD, and served the Baals and the Ashtoreths, the gods of Syria, the gods of Sidon, the gods of Moab, the gods of the people of Ammon, and the gods of the Philistines; and they forsook the LORD and did not serve Him" (Jdg 10:6). The Philistines also captured the arc of the Covenant in battle (1Sa 4:11) and place it alongside their idol Dagon, the fish God (1Sa

5:2), causing God in His wrath to destroy the fish god (1 Sa 5:4). The hand of the Lord was heavy on the people of Ashdod (one of the five Lords of the Philistines (Jos 13:3)), and He ravaged them and struck them with tumors (1 Sa 5:6).

CHAPTER 7. CONCLUSION

As we have seen throughout this study, to conclude that the Old Testament's accounts of war and violence are a reflection of God's character is a logical fallacy, for it ignores the fact that death is the natural consequence of sin throughout the Old and New Testaments. A nuanced reading of the Scriptures demonstrates that the wages of sin is death, yet out of the sea of death we find characters who are redeemed through faith in both the Old and New Testaments. Meanwhile, peoples are destroyed as a punishment for sin and sinful abominations, for attacking the Israelites, for blocking the Israelites from realizing God's will and from inheriting the Promised Land.

www.ingramcontent.com/pod-product-compliance
Lightning Source LLC
Chambersburg PA
CBHW060950050426
42337CB00052B/3405